Blogging for Fun and Profit

By Bob Cohen

bobology is a trademarks of Cohen-Naglestad Enterprises, LLC.

January 2021

www.bobology.com

Introduction

Blogging for Fun and Profit is for beginning to intermediate Bloggers. We'll learn what blogs are, what makes blogging unique, and some of the relationships between social networking sites like Facebook and blogs. I'll let you know the most popular current blogging software tools and where to find them on the web.

This book and the corresponding class taught at community colleges can be used by itself as an independent learning activity or taken as part of a series of classes and their workbooks on marketing.

For more in-depth information, you can read these books or take the courses:

- Introduction to Internet Marketing Methods
- Marketing with Facebook and Social Media
- Search Engine, Google Ads, Email, and E-Commerce Marketing

In the section on "How to Create a Blog," there are step-by-step instructions for using what I think is the easiest blogging website, Blogger, which also happens to be free to use for creating as many blogs as you like. We'll learn how to create a Google account (free), create a blog, and start posting and adding content to our blog. After we cover the basics of creating a blog, I'll cover how to manage blog settings, moderate comments, and control a blog's privacy.

Since blogs are about content, I'll give you some tips and ideas for finding content, coming up with ideas for blog topics, and some shortcuts for creating quick and easy blog posts.

If your goal is to make money with your blog, I'll cover ways to generate income from a blog with ads, affiliate programs, and writing for blogs. If you're creating a blog for an existing business, I'll show how a blog can help you with business development and internal communications..

Blog Basics

Whether you're new to blogging, an experienced Blogger, or website user, let's review a few basics of blogging. If you have more experience, feel free to skip to the sections that will help you most.

Why Blog?

I believe a blog is important and makes the best website for almost anyone or any organization. Blogs offer a few things that other types of websites don't offer or make easy to accomplish.

A blog makes adding and editing content easy with WYSIWYG (what you see is what you get) writing and publishing tools.

Blogs make search engines (like Google) happy. Every headline is a type of HTML (Hypertext Markup Language) format that search engines like. Blogs have lots of text for search engines to index. Because blogs are easier to update than traditional websites an actively updated blog receives a higher ranking in search engine results.

Blogs connect your content to the social web with a built-in RSS feed. Using the built-in RSS (I'll explain RSS in more detail later), your blog posts can be sent from your blog to social media sites like Twitter and Facebook automatically, saving you time by eliminating the need to post in two places.

Blog sites are easily managed by people with no programming or web design experience. A blog gives you the ability to make money with advertising and e-commerce. You can manage your design, layout, and other settings with point and click ease.

Blogs adapt their appearance when viewed on a smartphone. This function, called "responsive," is the site's ability to detect whether a visitor is using a desktop/laptop or a smartphone/tablet with a smaller screen. The blog automatically chooses the best format to display for the viewer based on what device they are using. My website, bobology.com, has a different appearance on smartphones than on a desktop and is a good example of how a responsive site changes its appearance.

What is a Blog?

A blog is an online periodical publication. Instead of a daily newspaper, an hourly news broadcast, a weekly television series, or a monthly magazine, a blog is published on the web.

It helps to look at blogs, read the content, and see how they're organized. The examples shown here are all blogs created by students who took "Blogging for Fun and Profit." A blog can be about any topic you want, as these examples show. The topics here include public transportation, associations, nonprofits, teaching, and small business, and you can find blogs on almost any topic that people are interested in following.

The term blog comes from a combination of web and log, which got combined into the term "blog." Blogs are a type of website, and all websites need to be available on the Internet at all times. As a result, blogs are almost always "hosted" by a service that provides blogging software and the Internet connection as a combined service. Later in the book, I'll give you a list of popular blogging services for both free and paid hosting so you'll know where to start your blog.

All websites, including blogs, are "hosted" on a computer with 24-hour access to the Internet. All text, photos, and other data are located on the computer where the blog is hosted. Blogs include web publishing, design, and layout tools, all of which are used with a standard web browser and don't require any programming knowledge or software on a computer.

Websites, including blogs, display information in a web browser (Internet Explorer, Firefox, Chrome, Safari, etc..). The software that manages the formatting and appearance of websites is called HTML, for Hypertext Markup Language. HTML includes instructions that web browsers interpret to display web pages. Other types of websites can be created with design tools or HTML and can be as simple as a single page or as complicated as a site like Amazon.com.

Blogs also include a built-in database to keep track of information in a chronological format. Like a ship captain's journal, a blog is a journal that includes information created by one or more authors. That information doesn't just have to be text; it can be any content displayed or used on the web, including photos, graphics, video, and audio. With a database, a blog is a website where the content can be indexed and searched. As a result, a blog is an extremely versatile type of website that's powerful yet easy to manage and use.

Where do you Find Blogs?

Where do you find blogs?

- Search sites:
  - Google
  - Yahoo, Bing, AOL, etc.
- Publications
  - Newspapers, magazines
  - Any periodical
- Social Network Sites
  - Twitter, Facebook, Instagram

Always look for the RSS icon on a website or the word "subscribe" and click to see if there is a feed.

Almost any publication or periodical on the web is a blog. Search sites like Google make finding blogs about any topic easy. Just add the term "blog" to any search, and you'll see a list of blogs.

Social networking sites often contain a blog within their functions, although many people don't think of social networks as blogs. Groups on Facebook, LinkedIn, and other social networking sites, status updates, and tweets are blog functions.

Always look for the RSS symbol or the word "subscribe" on a website. When you see either of these, the website is more than likely a blog since it has an RSS feed, which is one characteristic of a blog.

Admin, Publisher, Editor, Author

Here is a screenshot of the National Geographic Magazine website, an online periodical. Blogs and newspapers are similar in many ways. What's important to remember about blogging is that it's all about the content. Newspapers and magazines are familiar with what it takes to attract attention and sell their publications. Subscribers who find the articles useful, valuable, and interesting will continue to buy and read the publication. If a reader doesn't receive value from a publication, you wouldn't expect them to continue reading an article, purchase a copy, or subscribe.

The same is true for blogging. A blog with high value and interesting content will find an audience. Readership translates into website traffic, which is why blogs can have a greater impact on traffic than a website that rarely or never gets updated.

As a blogger, you are managing a publication on the web that is similar in many ways to a newspaper or other periodical. You have several roles in managing your periodical.

As the administrator, you control the blog's appearance, and as the publisher, you manage the organization and business functions; as an editor, you manage the content and what is published, and as the author, you create the content.

A blog is your website, and you make decisions about who can comment and what comments to publish, just like an editor chooses letters to the editor. You have an electronic publication without the cost of printing or mailing.

What's Different About a Blog?

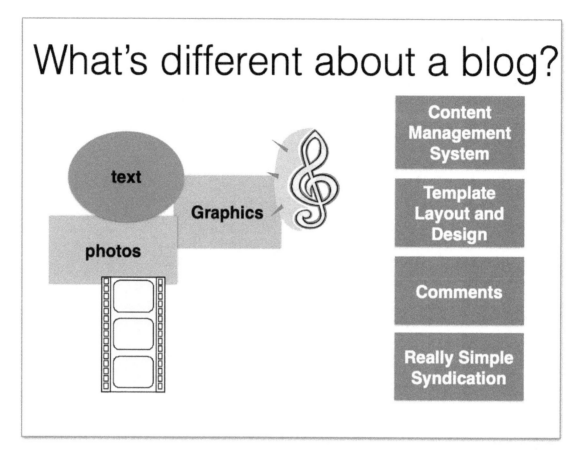

There are some characteristics of a blog that makes it different from other types of websites. These are the database, template, periodical, Really Simply Syndication (RSS), and comments. Let's look at each of these.

Database

With their built-in database, blogs are Content Management Systems. Your published content is stored in a database where your site can access it and change what displays on the viewer's screen. What appears in a browser changes based on how the website manages the database and content. This capability separates the content from the way the content is displayed, using a template to format the visible website's layout and design. The blog's software manages how the information contained in the blog's database files appears on the web page. Some of the types of displayed files are text, images or graphics, media, which can include audio (audio blogs are commonly known as podcasts), and video. The blogging software organizes all of this content and the layout, links, and files necessary for the website to function.

Template

All blogs include tools for managing the appearance of the site when it is displayed on a browser. Using point and click tools, you can control the layout and design. Layout refers to where information appears while design manages the color scheme, fonts, and other design aspects. You control layout and design using predefined templates that can be customized.

Periodical

A key element that makes a blog different from other websites is the chronological log index. The blog's author creates a periodical publication that files the articles according to the date and time in the blog's database. Readers can see the date and time any article was published, just like any periodical publication. Blogs can include standard webpages, which makes a blog a versatile way to create almost any website. Since blogs are so easy for a non-technical person to use, I recommend that anyone start a blog to see if it meets their website's needs. It often does, and a blog can make a quick, attractive, and easy to manage a website.

Really Simple Syndication (RSS)

Another thing that makes blogs different from other types of websites, and that's called RSS. All blogs come equipped with a technology called Really Simple Syndication. This is the technology that has made the web social and allows websites to connect, automatically pulling updated content from one website (the "feed") and displaying it on another website (the "reader").

Comments

Blogs allow readers to comment on articles. Like letters to the editor of a newspaper or other publication, blogs include the author's capability to allow and publish comments on articles. Don't worry. Although the capability exists, every blog includes the option to allow or not allow comments and to review any comment before it's published.

RSS

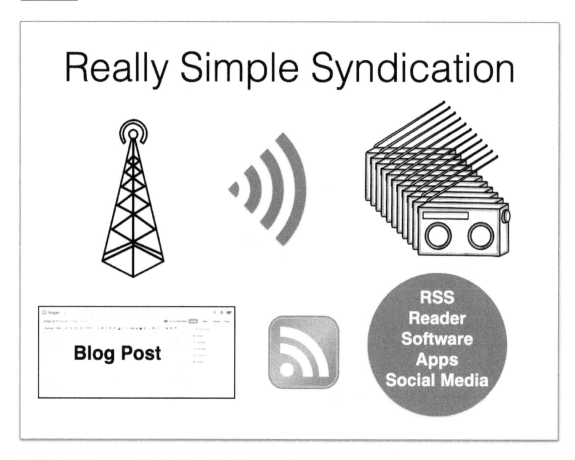

RSS, which stands for Really Simple Syndication, is a technology used on the web, primarily by blogs, to broadcast a blog's updates to the Internet. People who subscribe to an RSS feed using an RSS "Reader" software will provide them with updates from the blog or website when new content is posted or updated. The RSS feed does not contain all of the new content, usually just a headline or a short set of keywords to help the subscriber determine if he wants to read more. If so, then clicking on the link for the article takes him to the blog or web page where the full article appears.

OK, I usually get some blank stares at this point in my classes when I start explaining RSS, so let's go into a little more explanation. I have a blog, www.bobology.com, and I write articles and "post" updates to my blog. You can see what I have written and visit the blog to check if there are any new articles, but this requires that you enter the website URL (www.bobology.com) into your browser to visit my blog.

This might be OK if you visited one or two blogs occasionally. But if you would prefer a simpler process, you can subscribe to my RSS "feed." To do this with a blog, you might see a "subscribe" link or an RSS Feed icon.

When you "subscribe" to the RSS feed, you don't get emails sent to you every time there is an update from the blog you subscribed to, but you do get to see at a glance a list of articles by using your RSS "Reader."

Think of RSS as the radio of the Internet. Like a radio, you need to have a broadcasting station that creates a broadcast. To listen, you need a radio receiver and the frequency for any station you want to hear so you can adjust the tuner to the right station. Radio also has an on and off switch. When your radio is off, it's silent. When it's on, you can hear the broadcast for any station you've got set on your tuner.

RSS is similar in many ways to the radio. Websites that broadcast RSS sends out updates across the Internet when new content is published. To receive the RSS broadcast, commonly called an RSS "Feed," you need an RSS radio, an RSS reader software for your computer or mobile device. It would help if you had the frequency, which is the website's RSS Feed link, usually shown with the RSS symbol on the website. When you open your RSS reader software or application, you can then view or "listen" to RSS feeds and view the latest updates from the websites.

Before the latest web browsers, you would have needed a separate application called an RSS Reader. Most web browsers and email applications come with built-in RSS Readers, so you don't need a separate application for your Newsreader. Also, mobile apps such as Feedly and Feedler make it easy to scan your RSS subscriptions while on the go.

Using RSS lets you catch up with updates and website subscriptions from any computer or mobile device that uses RSS reader apps. Using RSS, it's possible to subscribe to many updates and view them when it's convenient for you. Besides, it doesn't clutter your email inbox with a new email.

Because social networking sites use RSS for their status updates, blogs have become the website of choice for anyone trying to publicize anything since all blogs come with RSS capabilities. Using RSS subscriptions also allows you to keep up with the latest news and updates from some of the Internet's best sources.

Your blog has a URL address for subscribing to the RSS feed, which will notify any subscriber when a new post is published.

Using RSS Tools

To connect your RSS posts to social networks, its best to use a third-party tool that automatically reposts your blog posts to social networks.

The most popular of these are:

- www.dlvr.it

- www.buffer.com

- www.hootsuite.com

- www.ifttt.com

Using these tools, you can enter the URL address of your blog and log in to your social networking accounts to have your posts appear on your social networks within minutes of being posted on your blog.

Note: Posts are the RSS content, while Pages are like any standard webpage.

Comments

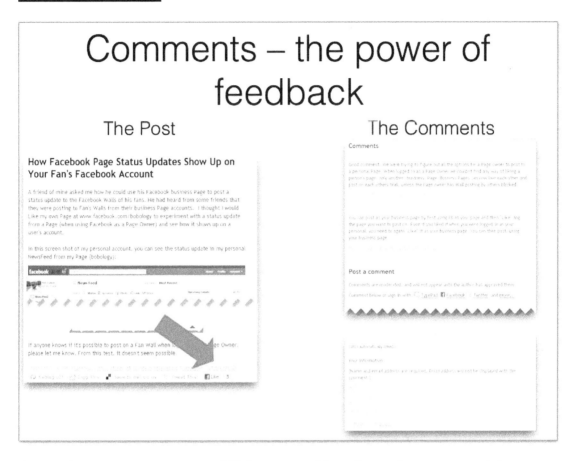

A post is any content you publish to your blog. It can be a text article, a single word, a link to another web page, a photo, an image, a video, an audio recording, a file, or any other content you choose to publish. The process of publishing content to your blog is called "posting." The term posting was first used when letters were mailed, and the process of putting a stamp and mailing was called posting. In web technology, the term has a similar meaning. To upload information to a web site is called posting. In blogging, any time you publish content, you are "posting" it to your blog.

If we take a look at this post example, you can see the title "How Facebook Page Status Updates Show Up on Your Fan's Facebook Account." I wrote this article when a friend asked me how his Facebook Page content would appear in the Facebook Newsfeed. At the bottom of the post, the blogging software shows two comments on this post. Every blogging software allows comments.

We'll discuss later in managing your blog settings how to control commenting since you have complete control over whether to:

- Allow comments or not for each post.

- Determine which comments appear and which don't.

- Decide who can and who cannot comment on your posts.

Comments

Clicking on the "comments" link opens a new window for making a comment, which is the usual way to comment on almost any blog. When a comment is made for a specific post and approved by the author, it's displayed for that post along with any other comments made on that post. Readers can scroll through the comments to review the comments, add a comment of their own, or reply to a comment that someone else made. The blog author can also reply to a comment with a comment, which is the usual practice for bloggers.

The interaction between the author and readers using comments creates a dialog and allows immediate feedback and participation on any discussion topic. Sometimes blogs require anyone commenting login and identify themselves. A user's screen name (which can be different than their real name) often appears next to the comment. The blog automatically places this information, along with the comment's time and date, with the correct blog post and stores it.

Comments and feedback are one of the keys to the community and social aspect of a blog. It's possible to create a post and not allow any comments, but comments show other readers that you have an audience that reads your posts and increases your credibility. Comments are available to read later, and a reader can catch up to speed on the topic and where the discussion ended.

The author of the post usually manages comments. Moderating comments is the way a blogger can review any comment before it appears. Comments usually appear at the bottom of the post they refer to and are in chronological order. Authors can respond to comments instead of editing the original post, which is the preferred method of responding because it doesn't alter the original article.

Since you're the publisher of your blog, it's completely up to you to choose whether or not to allow comments on your posts. You've become the editor of your web publication, and comments are the "letters to the editor" for your publication. You have complete control of all comment activity, which we will discuss in the administrative tools section of this book.

Layout and Design with Templates

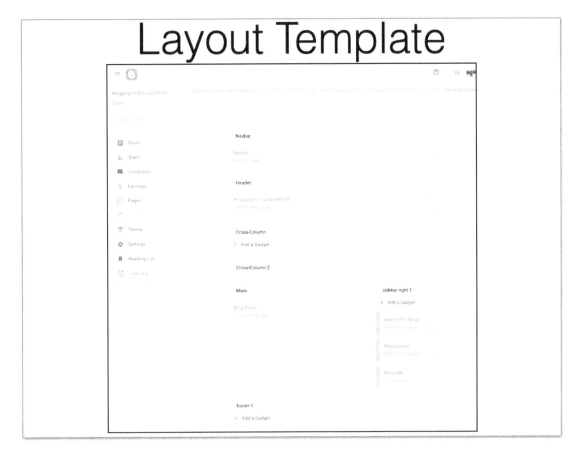

To see what makes a blog work, let's look at the software that manages a blog. What you see here is a screenshot of the "layout" template of the blog. The layout function is used to control the appearance and shows the placeholders for various blog parts.

Blogs and websites use a web programming language called Cascading Style Sheets (CSS). A style sheet is used to manage a consistent style, just like a word processing document. The style sheet contains all the HTML code for a style and creates a template, so every page on the blog has the same style, layout, and appearance.

The layout consists of defined spaces on the blog page that function as containers and holds portions of the blog content. One of the great features of blogs is that style sheets can be customized and modified, so it's easy to add, delete, and change the container layout. Once the container layout changes, the style sheet makes sure, all the blog pages use the same layout. All blogs include many pre-designed styles and templates for you to use, so you can pick a design without knowing any CSS.

Depending on the blogging software, these containers are called "gadgets," "page elements," "widgets," or "design elements" (they all mean the same thing). The blogging software will determine your container's exact size and shape to display properly on a web browser and fill it with the correct content from the blog database. The advantage of using CSS and this container approach is that you can maintain the same style on every page of the blog and only need to be concerned about which containers you want to use.

Gadgets and Widgets

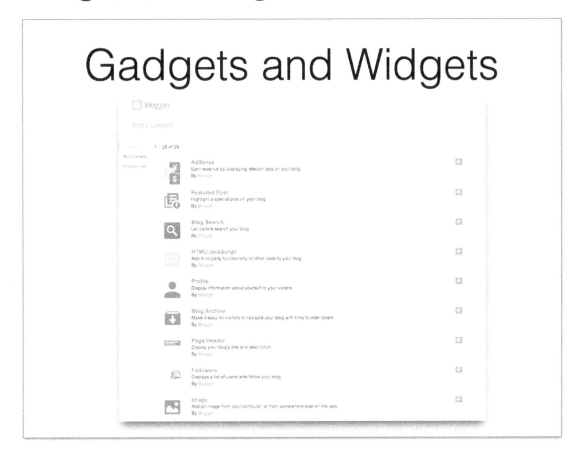

Standard containers used on almost every blog include the header, blog post content, the archive (a list of the posts), and a footer. Most blogs have styles for one, two, three, and four-column layout and features to add and edit gadgets.

There are over 1,000 gadgets for Blogger, including predesigned HTML, to display information in the gadget container. Clicking on the Add Gadget link when using the design function brings up a list of gadgets you can use in your blog. A very popular gadget is the Google AdSense gadget, which displays Google AdWords and enables you to make money when people click on ads displayed in the gadget.

You can get "under the hood" of the software with the actual software code, so for anyone who knows how to program or wants to learn, it's possible to modify anything. But for the rest of us, blogging software makes it easy to create and manage a blog without the need to learn how to program.

Blog Appearance

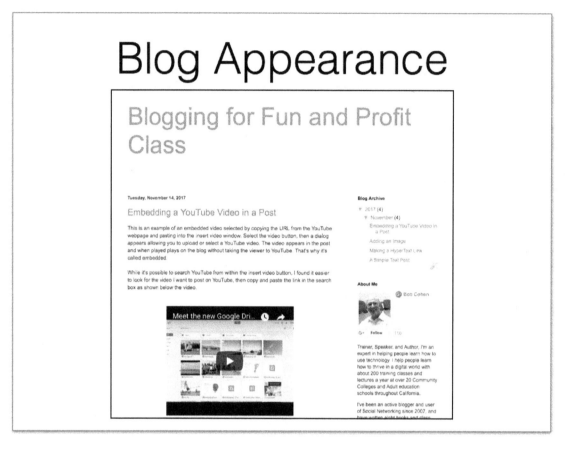

While the layout template shows the gadgets and widgets in a row and column format, your blog will only show the content in the areas you've chosen to display.

If you have an empty gadget, nothing will appear in that space when viewed in a browser. The blogging software is doing its work for you by placing the content you've chosen in the right position on your site, automatically adjusting the amount of space necessary.

Each page of your blog will display the same layout. If you want to have some pages of your blog appear with a different layout, you'll have to use one of the other blogging services with that feature.

I recommend you edit, add, and remove a gadget or two, move them around in position, and then look at how it affects your website's appearance. With Blogger, once you have a layout with the gadgets you want, it can be modified without affecting your blog's content unless you have customized the layout with your own code. It's possible to modify almost anything in Blogger with custom code, but the drag-and-drop layout features are more than enough for almost all users.

Theme or Design

When a blog displays in a browser (Edge, Firefox, Safari, Chrome, etc.), you see many items on the web page. These include the URL, or Uniform Resource Locator, graphics, text, and other content. A Header, or title, is usually a standard part of any blog and contains your blog's name. Often a short one or two-line description. It's best not to change the title once you've created it since it appears in search engine results. Don't worry about the appearance of your blog title for now since you can replace it with a custom graphic at any time.

The blogging software uses the design choices in your template to control the columns, and the "gadgets" displayed. Each gadget, also referred to as a widget, or page element is a placeholder in the blog software for you to use in your design. Gadgets are pre-formatted and sized so that they will automatically fit in your blog where you place them. By separating the content of the gadget from the layout, a blog gives you the ability to customize your design.

Blogger's theme designer gives you choices to customize your background, layout, colors, fonts, and more. In most blogging software, including

Blogger, template colors and fonts can be edited for a more customized appearance.

Before customizing any template design, be sure you're happy with that template since customizations like color and font changes are usually lost when switching from one template to another.

Test Blog

One way to experiment with themes and layout is to set up a "test' blog that's private and only you can see. I'll explain in administration how to set up your test blog and hide it from search and viewing.

Social Networking

Social networking is important to mention because everyone's free social network account also includes a free blog. A user with an account on Facebook, the most popular social networking site, can do all their communication without going outside of their account. Social network sites include mail, messaging, photo sharing, video, blogging, and other functions.

Social networking adds the networking element to all these communications, making it easy to find people you know, celebrities, businesses, and organizations.

Blogs are a form of social networking since they allow for creating a community through feedback and comments. The ability to post comments is typically part of every social networking application.

Facebook uses a blogging function, RSS, to send communications between Friends and Fans. When you connect with a Friend, Facebook will automatically send them any post you make on your Facebook page. You can see all of your posts on your Profile page.

Your Home page for Facebook includes a "News Feed." The News Feed shows all the news (which are posts they have made) from your Friends and Fan pages that you follow and some other notification information Facebook sends users. Facebook integrates many blog functions in your account. Your "Timeline" on Facebook is basically a blog where you can post, or publish, content, and people can comment on it. Facebook brings social networking capability to connect you to a network of people. Using a blog, people need to find your blog in the first place to find your content.

Facebook and Blogs

Facebook integrates many blog functions. Your "Timeline," formerly called the "Wall," in Facebook is basically a blog where you can post, or publish, content, and people can comment on it. Facebook brings social networking capability to connect you to a network of people. Using a blog, people need to find your blog in the first place to find your content.

So would anyone need a blog that has a Facebook (or any social media site) account?

These are some of the main reasons why:

- Facebook controls the layout and features you can use; you can control much more on a blog.

- Facebook manages all the advertising; on a blog, you can sell advertising.

- Facebook requires you to use applications written for Facebook; on a blog, you can use a wider variety of tools.

- Your blog can have its own domain name (bobology.com); on Facebook, all accounts are facebook.com/youraccountname.

- Blogs can be used as a central location to publish to Facebook and other sites using RSS.

- Blogs are better for making money with affiliate programs and commerce.

- Organizations, businesses, and brands (including a celebrity or public figure) use Pages on Facebook with Fans.

Since Facebook allows you to connect with people easily but doesn't give you the site management you may want with a blog, an effective approach is to use Facebook (and other social networking sites) as a way to help drive traffic to your blog.

Other Social Networks

Facebook is the largest social network on the Internet, but it isn't the only one. Just as people like different types of food, people like different types of social networks. For people who like short messages, there's Twitter. For photos on Instagram, for bookmarking pictures from web pages, there's Pinterest, and for professional networking, there's LinkedIn. Social networks are popular because they allow people to join, connect, and share information with other users. I recommend you try several of them to find the ones you like to use, and using a social network could be your way of expressing yourself. If so, you don't really need a blog.

Social Media Strategies

If you're using social media to drive traffic to your blog, here are some strategies I recommend from my Secrets of Internet Marketing book:

- Facebook: Photos for fans to share
- Twitter: Niche authority or timely promotions
- LinkedIn: B2B with group ownership or activity
- YouTube: 2-minute videos
- Pinterest: Photos with links

Instagram: product and business photos.

Starting Your Blog

What to Blog About?

While not essential, it helps to have a goal and theme in mind before creating a blog. You can use your imagination and freedom to share your thoughts about anything, be as specific as you want, or ramble on. You can even create a fictional blog, pretending to be a character, and write under a pseudonym.

Most blogging sites, including Blogger, allow you to create multiple blogs at no or little additional charge. I recommend that you think about a focus or theme for your blog. It's not as important for a personal blog that only your friends and family might view, but for a business or a topical blog, it helps to stay "on topic."

As you develop an audience of readers, they will come to expect articles and content related to your theme or topic. Sticking to a theme doesn't mean that you can't mingle in personal observations or go off-topic once in a while, though. Relating a personal story or a post on something about yourself gives your readers a chance to know you better. In fact, blogging has become popular because people can get to know other people better through the Internet.

Blogger's Block

Surveys show that the fear of speaking in public is the most common fear people have. Just like speaking in public, posting content on the web can cause fear in people. There's no one solution to publishing and posting content. I recommend to clients to use as natural a voice as possible to communicate on the web. Don't think of the web as an anonymous group of people. Think of one person at a time and what you would say to them.

We all have some social interaction in our personal and professional lives, and we all share more information in public already than what might seem apparent. You've probably written an email to a friend, taken a photo that you shared with people, maybe you are an engaging conversationalist, or you are out and about during the day.

The key is that people rarely keep all of their personal life out of their professional life, and they rarely keep all of their professional life out of their personal life. People talk to their family about work and family, and personal issues come up during work conversations. Think about customers or clients who get to know your personality, they probably like doing business with you because they like you, and they've probably gotten to know more about your life as a result. It's this person that needs to be captured and presented on your blog for your web presence.

Where Do You Get a Blog?

Blogs consist of software that runs the blog and a hosted location where the blog is made available to the Internet. The software, like Blogger, manages the content, layout, and settings. To be available on the Internet, the blog software needs to be installed on a computer that is always connected to the Internet, or a "host."

It's possible to host your blog if you have a computer with the right technical requirements for hosting a website. But this usually involves a more expensive Internet connection than most of us have at home. It requires the technical expertise to host a web site, keep it secure from malware and spam, and always keep the computer powered. It's much easier to use the free and paid blog hosting services to do all of this work for you. Some web designers create their websites on blogs and provide hosting services for their clients.

Free sites offer a lot of functions and are more than adequate for many users. Paid ones offer more templates, online help, data storage, video, audio, and add-ons. If one of your goals is to generate revenue from blogging, you will eventually want your own paid blog site.

Everything you learn on Blogger will help you use any other blogging site, and if your goal is to publish content, Blogger will meet your needs, and it's priced right without any costs.

- Blogger www.blogger.com
- WordPress www.wordpress.com
- TypePad www.typepad.com
- GoDaddy or other hosted WordPress Hosting www.godaddy.com
- Squarespace www.squarespace.com
- Shopify www.shopify.com
- Wix www.wix.com
- Weebly www.weebly.com

Blogger

Free and easy to use blogging website.

WordPress

Specialized templates and plugins for almost any type of site function. However, it requires you to update and manage your software and can be over complex for beginners. Supported WordPress hosting can be expensive.

TypePad

A full feature blogging tool with hosting includes technical support, audio and file hosting, advanced image editing with Adobe Aviary as part of all plans and features for full customization. Has a plan with unlimited storage and blogs.

Squarespace

Offers an integrated blog, shopping cart, and beautiful themes and technical support. Allows uploading of audio, files, built-in forms, integration with MailChimp. One of the few to include the option for password-protected content areas. Has a fee for each domain name site.

Shopify

Primarily a shopping cart for e-commerce but has a fun featured blog. If you plan to sell many products, I'd recommend looking into Shopify. However, you can integrate your Shopify store with any blog on a separate page and use the individual to buy now buttons for products in any post or page.

Wix and Weebly

Wix and Weebly, while not originally blogs, have added an RSS feature that supports posts similar to blogging. These services started as small business website hosting tools that created and hosted a site simple for small businesses. With the need to market on social media, they both added RSS posting to their services. If you already have a site hosted with any service that includes RSS, there's no need to change. Just start using the posting feature to get the benefit of blogging on your website.

Import and Export

Blogs can also be exported and imported from one service to another. Virtually all the text, images, pages, and posts will be moved over since the blog content is actually in a database. Most of the popular blogging services use a similar format for the blog data.

Self Hosting a WordPress Blog

WordPress is a popular blogging tool. WordPress software is called "open source" and is free for anyone to use. As a result, web hosting companies often offer WordPress blogging software since they don't have to pay a fee for the software. Web designers often use WordPress to create websites since blogs allow a publisher to create web pages and never even use the blog's journal functions. It's freely available from http://www.wordpress.org. As a result of being open source, WordPress has the widest selection of templates and widgets of any blogging software, which is one reason for its popularity. It accounts for almost 50% of the blogging software because many web designers also use WordPress for developing websites.

Some reasons you may want to use WordPress include templates that offer you the functionality such as membership programs, or a plugin that gives you additional features only available for WordPress.

For the new blogger, WordPress can be intimidating. Because it's developed and maintained by a more technical user community, it's a more complex blogging software to use. WordPress.com is a company that hosts WordPress sites but with pre-selected plugins and templates.

Many options and settings give a user great control over a blog. Sometimes, however, the options can be overwhelming and not even necessary for a blog. Once you learn Blogger, which is easy to learn and versatile, all blog software will be easier for you to learn.

There are some important aspects of using WordPress to consider. When using the open-source WordPress software from www.wordpress.org, the user or website manager (you) handle managing and administrating the software.

Updating Software

As new versions of WordPress are issued, the administrator's job is to update the software and load it on the hosting site. The administrator also has to manage all add-ons, templates, and widgets and obtain the software and install them in the WordPress software. Unless you're comfortable with this technology, it's best left to a professional web manager or hosting company. Most hosting companies only make WordPress available for your use but don't actively support WordPress software. I don't recommend hosting your WordPress site unless you are up to managing software.

Supported WordPress Hosting

GoDaddy (www.godaddy.com) and other WordPress hosting sites now offer some form of supported WordPress. At the time of publishing, GoDaddy offered:

- automatic updates for WordPress (not for plugins or add-ons)

- daily backup of your entire site

- additional security

Essential Plugins for WordPress

Several critical plugins are necessary to install if you are using WordPress, and these are:

- Backup - your hosting service will not likely backup your site for you

- Anti-Spam for Comments - without a spam filter, you'll receive many more comments

- Security - since WordPress is open-source software, many hackers go to the wp-admin page to see if they can hack the site

Here are my recommended plugins for these functions:

- Backup: www.backup-guard.com

- Anti-Spam Comment Filter: Akismet, available from www.wordpress.com

- Security: BackupBuddy at www.ithemes.com

Creating a Blog with Blogger

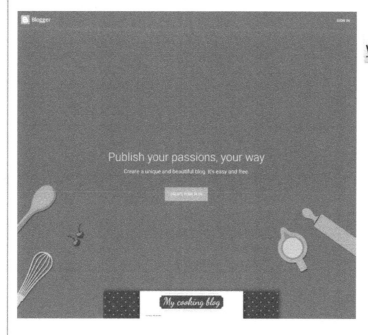

For the beginner, I recommend learning with Google's blogging software, Blogger. It's easy to get started, easy to use, and allows you to run Google's ads. It has a good selection of widgets, which are called Gadgets on Blogger. Blogger continually creates updates and makes changes to add new features and functions to their site, adding more features and options.

Blogger allows you to create as many blogs as you like, but it's up to you to keep up with them. You can also delete any blog you create.

Step 1 - Create a Google Account

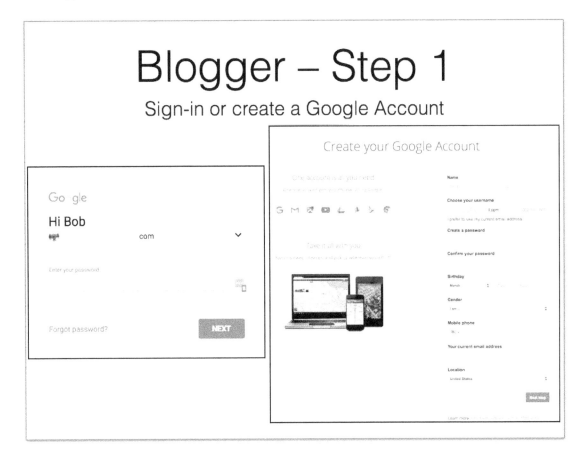

Your first step is to go to www.blogger.com and select Get Started. If you don't have a Google user account, you'll need to create one. Its free so go ahead.

You'll need do the the following steps:

1. Enter your email address (you don't need a gmail account, any email address will work)

2. Retype your email address (this confirms and corrects any mistakes in typing)

3. Enter a password

4. Retype your password

Step 2 - Name Your Blog

When coming up with a name for your blog, I recommend starting with anything you like. It's easy to change the name later, and services like Blogger will let you create multiple blogs.

Your blog's name will not be the same as its URL. Your blog's name will be its title, like for a newspaper. The URL, on the other hand, will be its actual location on the Internet. To understand the difference, let's take a quick look at some basic terminology.

URLs, Domain Names, and IP Addresses Explained

URL stands for Uniform Resource Locator, a code for finding an exact page on the Internet. The entire string of letters and numbers in a browser's address bar is a URL. You may have noticed that these can be short, or they can be long. The Internet has a lot of content, so you need a pretty big code to name each page.

Luckily, there are Domain Names, also called Domains for short. A Domain is your blog's address on the Internet. It can be, but it doesn't have to be similar to your title, and it's best for branding if it's a short, easy to remember address that anyone can type into a web browser's address bar.

Typing the URL address sends a command from your computer to the Internet's computers, requesting that a copy of the web page for the URL you typed be delivered back to your computer. Your computer then displays the web page in your browser window.

Subdomain

A subdomain is a subdivided domain, much like a subdivided building. A building can use one street mailing address and be divided into individual apartments or offices with different tenants. Each occupant has their own space but uses the building's street mailing address with an apartment or suite number. Domains can be subdivided in much the same way.

The domain owner (like the building owner) can subdivide the domain into individual spaces with separate occupants. A domain name to the left of .blogspot is a subdomain you create when you create your blog. You can't use a subdomain name that's already in use, much like you can't use someone's email address name if they've already claimed it on Gmail, Hotmail, or other mail services.

Business Domains

It's possible to register a domain name for your website in blogger or use a domain name you already have and make your blogger blog your website. Where you host your website and where you register your domain name are independent of each other. It's possible to use a domain name for a blog or any other type of website.

If you want to establish brand recognition or make your blog your business website, then using your own domain name is recommended. It's always possible to register a new domain or assign an existing domain name to your blog at any time after you create it. Still, your setup usually will use the blog hosting service domain to start with, then ask you to assign or register your domain name.

Step 3 Select a Starter Template

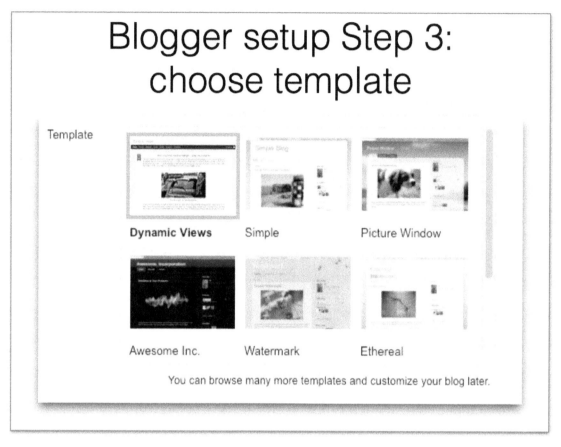

Your Blogger Template

Blogger and almost all blogging software provide a selection of templates to make it easy to design and layout your blog. It's always possible to change your template and customize your blog later, so I don't recommend spending too much time choosing a template when getting started.

The template for a blog controls the design and layout of the blog's appearance. This concept separates the design elements, or template, from the content displayed on the blog. The content will include your blog post copy and images and information on every page as part of your design. For example, each page will have your blog's title, some standard gadgets like the archive and about me gadgets, and your blog posts. These are standard template design placeholders that will appear on every page of your blog. Additional content will appear as a header, footer, or in a column, based on the type of content gadget you select for your layout.

Your template design controls your blog appearance, and every page of your blog will appear with the colors, layout, text size, and text style from your template. Using templates allows bloggers to concentrate on content and still provides a range of choices in design. Blogger includes an ever-expanding choice of templates for you to start with, all of which can be customized for your own style.

Changing Templates

Blogger offers an increasing selection of templates for your design. You'll need to choose one here to continue to set up your blog, but you can change your template anytime. I recommend trying different templates after getting some blog content on your blog to see how the appearance changes. It's better to choose your template first, then customize it. Any customization you do for background colors, font styles, or other changes is usually lost when you change from one template to another. I recommend you experiment with templates until you find one you like, then make any changes.

When you make a template change, all of your content is kept the same. Just the layout, typefaces, and colors change. This includes posts, comments, photos, files, audio, and graphics. You are only changing the look and style of your blog when you change templates.

Choose a Domain - Optional

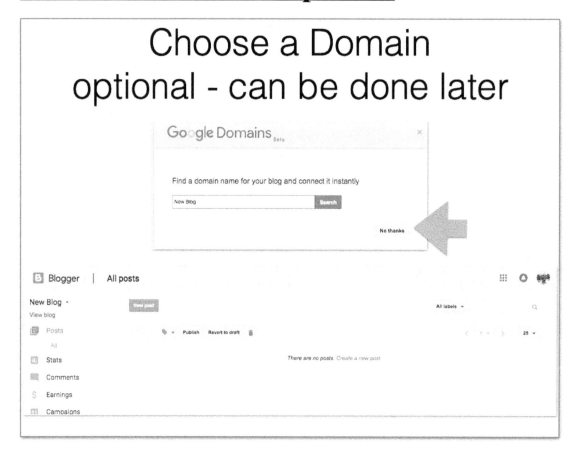

You can use Blogger's sub-domains for free, but Google is also a place where you can register your domain name if you want. Domain names are part of your internet branding, and if you want to make it easier for people to find you on the Web by giving them a domain name, by all means, register one.

You can also use a domain name you've registered with any other service. Your domain name is yours to use as long as you pay the annual fee (about $10-15). Registering a domain name and hosting your website are two different services so that you can have your domain name registered with one company and your website hosted with another.

You can always go to Blogger settings to register a domain later or point a domain you already have registered to your Blogger website. Once you use a domain for your blog, the sub-domain, blogspot.com, no longer appears on the internet.

Using Blogger

Your Login Screen

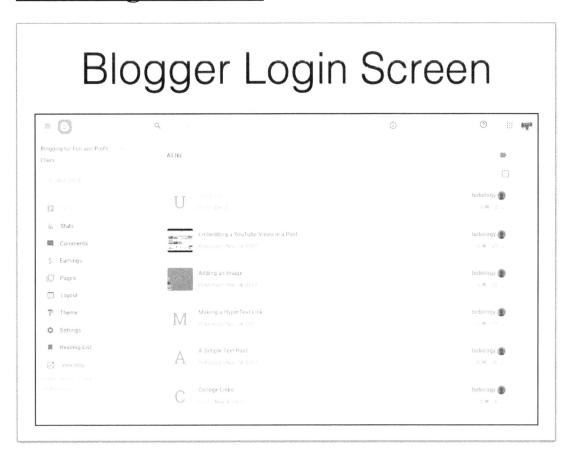

When you want to return to your blog to create posts or manage options, go to Blogger.com and enter your google username and password. You'll see the administrative page for the blog you've created.

If you only have one blog, you'll see a column of options on the left and a list of posts to the right. This screen will appear whenever you log in.

If you have multiple blogs, you'll see a drop-down arrow to the right of your blog name. Click on the arrow to access any blog you've create on Blogger. The name of the blog will change to help you see what blog you're currently working on.

If you want to create a new blog, scroll down to New Blog at the bottom to select it. Let's learn how to create a new blog for testing things out. I've found that having a test blog is an excellent way to experiment with templates, HTML code and trying things out before doing them on your public blog as you learn how to use the tools. Let's get started.

Creating a Test Blog

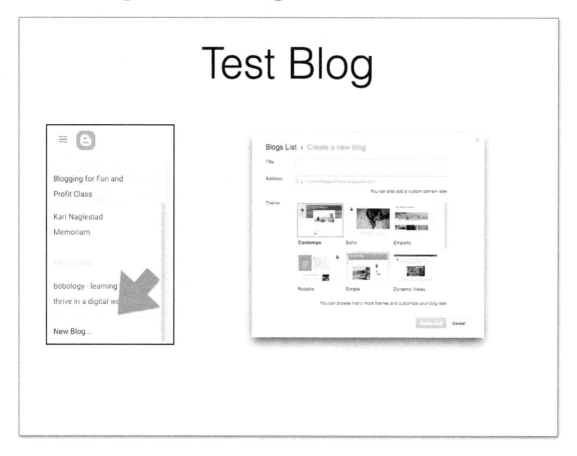

When logged into Blogger, select the drop-down arrow to the right of your blog name in the upper left corner of the screen.

- Then select the New Blog menu item at the bottom.
- Enter a title - this can be any text, so use Test Blog if you want. Then enter an address for your URL address.
- Choose any template; you'll be using this blog to try out different designs and layouts anyway.
- When prompted to register a domain skip that step; this is a test blog.

Test Blog Settings

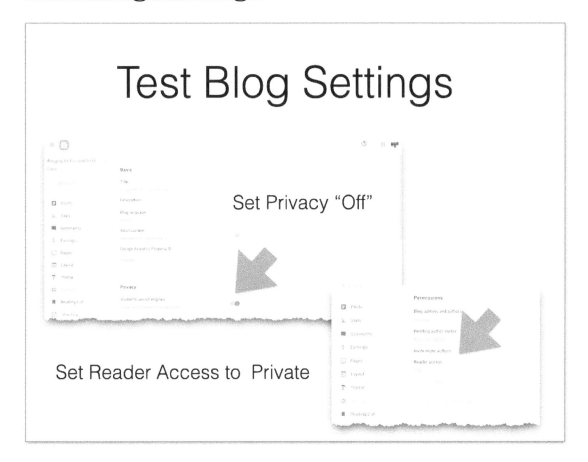

Once you've created your blog, you'll want to hide it so no one can see it on the internet.

Here's how to hide your blog so only you can see it on the Web:

- When your blog admin screen appears, select Settings in the left column.

- Change Privacy

  - In the Basic section, set Privacy to OFF

- Change Reader Access to Private.

  - Save your changes.

The only person who can see it is you since you are the author, and it's hidden from search and Blogger listings. Even if someone accidentally finds your blog address, they won't be able to see it and will see a screen requiring a Google account login.

Adding Posts to Your Blog

In this section I'll go over using the New Post feature to add text, images, and videos to your blog. Think of each post as similar to an issue of a magazine or newsletter. Each post is it's own article and every post creates a new webpage for your blog.

Posting and Editing

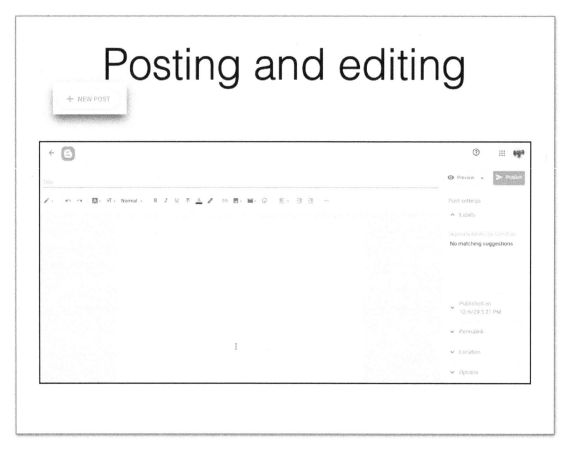

WYSIWYG and HTML Editor

Blogger and most other blogging tools use an editor to do both WYSIWYG (What You See Is What You Get) and HTML (Hypertext Markup Language).

Using the WYSIWYG view means when you start typing, your text appears just as it is when you publish your post. A WYSIWYG editor provides an easier way to create posts than HTML, and there's no need to know HTML commands for formatting.

HTML is the code that web browsers interpret to display a web page on a computer or mobile device. An HTML editor uses the actual HTML code to edit the content and requires knowledge of the syntax to format your web page's appearance. With knowledge of HTML software and code commands, the post content can be edited using HTML by selecting the HTML tab on the editor screen.

Blogger automatically defaults to the WYSIWYG editor (called Compose view in Blogger) when the new post window opens. The WYSIWYG editor looks like a standard word processor and works similarly to computer word processing software.

There aren't as many editing options in a WYSIWYG editor as on a full word processor for font styles, sizes, layout, and other options you might like using. This is because HTML has to use some standards that all computers (PC, Mac, etc.) and different browsers (Edge, Mozilla, Safari, Chrome, etc.) can display, so the web page looks the same regardless of what computer or browser someone is using.

The WYSIWYG editor's features cover the majority of a user's needs for creating posts. However, to get a certain layout, image size, or font, it may be necessary to create a blog post in HTML and then cut and paste it into your blog. Simple HTML editors are not very difficult, and I'll cover some options later.

You might want to use HTML when you copy and paste HTML code from another web service into your blog. PayPal, shopping carts, email subscription forms, maps, affiliate links are examples of services that give you HTML code that you can copy and paste into your content.

Top Row Buttons and Fields

Back

The back arrow returns you to the dashboard screen. If you accidentally forget to save your work, Blogger asks you to save it before leaving.

Title

Across the top, from left to right, Blogger's editor displays a text field for entering your post title, required for all posts. Blogs automatically assign a new web page to each post, using the blog title in the URL.

Preview

To the right of the title is a button for Preview, with a drop-down arrow option to save your post. The Save button saves your post without publishing it to the web for review and editing. Blogger automatically saves your posts as drafts about once every 20-30 seconds, preventing any accidental loss of work progress.

Publish

Used to publish your post to your blog and make it visible on the web.

Spell Checker Icon

You can use your web browser's spell checker or use add-on spell checkers like grammarly.com

Using the WYSWYG Editor

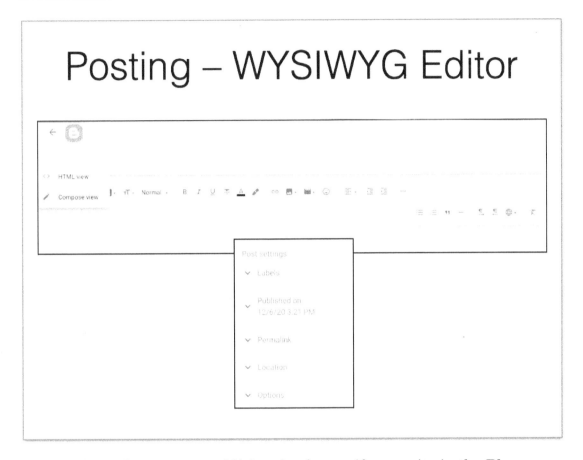

You don't need to use any additional software if you write in the Blogger editor. Let's go over the editing tools, which will create HTML formatted webpages.

Below the blog name and title line are some additional buttons and icons. Most of these are formatting options that can be applied to text when selected and highlighted for editing.

Pen

The Pen icon with the drop-down arrow gives you the option to switch from Compose view to HTML and back.

Editing Icons

To the right of the pen icon from left to right, the icons are:

- Undo - Undoes the last action.
- Redo - Redoes the last action.
- Font Selection - Displays a list of fonts available.
- Font Size Selection - Changes the font size.

- Paragraph Style - Changes the paragraph style to HTML compliant choices.

- Bold - Bolds the selected text.

- Italic - Italicizes the selected text.

- Underline - Underlines the selected text.

- Strikethrough - strikes a line through the selected text.

- Text Color - Applies a new color to the selected text.

- Text Background Color - Applies a background color to the selected text.

- Link - For creating Hypertext Links (covered later).

- Insert Image - Click to open up the upload photo option, then select a photo or image from your computer to publish.

- Insert Video - Click to open the embed/link to video option, then paste a video URL link.

- Insert Special Characters - Displays special symbols and emoticons for insertion at your cursor location.

More (...)

- Justification - Left, center, or right alignment of selected text.

- Indent - Indents the text one tab at a time.

- Outdent - Moves the text back one indent at a time.

- Bullet list - Creates a bullet list from lines of the selected lines of text.

- Numbered list - Creates a numbered list of the selected lines of text.

- Quote - Applies a style that indents the text left and right.

- Page Break - inserts a page break on the home page for the post. Text and images above the break appear on the home page of your blog with the "read more" link below for readers to view the full post.

- Left to Right paragraph - applies paragraphs that start on the left for reading text left to right, the standard for U.S. users.

- Right to Left Paragraph - moves paragraph format to Right to Left.

- Language - select another language for this post.

- Clear formatting - used when cutting and pasting from Word or other sources to remove all formatting.

Post Settings

On the right side of the editor, below Post settings, are links for Labels, Schedule, Permalink, Location, and Options.

- Labels applies a category label for a post, which can be used for indexing and creating a list of topics for users to find. For example, a blog about fruit would use apples, oranges, and pears as labels. A post would be assigned a label, then visitors could search for posts by the label category.

- Published on - use this option for scheduling when a post will be published

- Permalink displays the URL address for the post you're editing and allows you to create a custom link, useful for making it easier to give out a URL address so people can remember it.

- Location - will display the location of a post using Google maps

- Options - choices for allowing or not allowing comments on each post.

Titles, Search Engines, and Blog Posts

As you create posts, you are adding pages to your site. As you get more involved in blogging start using keywords in your headlines, which become part of your URL and help in search engine optimization. Every post creates a web page added to your site, using the title as part of the page's URL.

Adding posts with keywords in the titles are key to search engines in two ways. First, to search engines, more web pages on your site means you have more content, including keywords. Update frequency is one factor used to rank your site's relevance for search results. Second, search engines look for titles relevant to a search. Search engines index all content on your blog and your post titles are considered more relevant content by search engines than the body text. Since each blog post you create results in a new web page, and a new title, a blog is a search engine "friendly" website.

Using Microsoft Word

You may lose formatting used in an application like Microsoft Word, so saving a Word file as a Rich Text or Plain Text file (.rtf or .txt) is important to be able to cut and paste content from Word into a blog editor. Word uses proprietary Microsoft formatting code to format text and layout while the web uses HTML code. A simpler tool like WordPad (included with all current Windows versions) is all the editor you need and it saves all files in the .rtf format, ready to copy and paste into your WYSIWYG editor.

Mac Users

Mac users can use Pages, which produces documents that can be copied and pasted into the WYSIWYG editor with minor reformatting required.

Post Results

Here's what the post looks like on the blog site after it's published.

All the layout and formatting is done for you without the need to know any HTML or programming. This blog's template selected the fonts and colors for the blog title, post titles, post text, background color, and the two-column layout.

The blog post's date and time are automatically added, and an archive is created, which indexes the blog posts by date. Besides posting text, there are other options for posting hypertext links, photos, images, and videos.

Hypertext Links

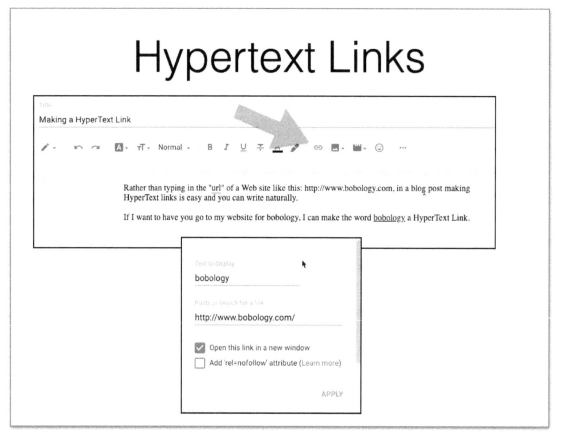

What is Hypertext?

Hypertext is a feature that provides a link to other web pages for text or graphics that appear on a web page. It's a great way to enrich the text and graphic content for your readers. Hypertext describes text and graphics that include a link to another web page. The information that makes the text or graphics a hypertext link doesn't appear on the web page but is included in the HTML code for the page, hidden from the reader.

When viewed in a browser, hypertext appears in a different color, usually blue, and is often underlined. Scrolling over causes the mouse cursor to change from an arrow to a hand. The term hypertext also applies to graphics, which can also include links to another web page hidden. With the WYSIWYG editor, it's easy to create hypertext links within your text and content. Photos and images can also be made into Hypertext links, but this is done using the photo button.

Creating Hypertext Links

To create a hypertext link, select the text using your mouse so it's highlighted. Click on the blue Link button in the WYSIWYG editor. A new window opens. Then type or paste in the URL (http://www.websitename.com) for the destination web page. Click on OK, and you'll have created a hypertext link. When you publish your post, the text you selected to link will usually appear blue in color (although that can depend on the browser and your blog template). When the reader of your blog scrolls their mouse over the text, the cursor changes appearance to indicate they can click on the text and view another page.

Blogger users will see the word "Link" to create a Hypertext link, while other blog editors use an icon of a globe with a chain link or just a chain link.

Your blog needs to know what web page you are linking to using this text, and the full URL of the web page is entered in the web address field. Remember to enter the full URL, including the "http://" all the way to the end of the .com, .edu, or another domain ending.

Blogger includes an option to test the link before saving, and I recommend you test every link to make sure it works. If the correct web page opens when tested, click on the OK button to save your hypertext link. Your HTML code is created for you automatically by the editor, and the text will appear as a hypertext link in the blog post when published.

Adding links in your blog posts creates an additional resource for the reader. By providing a direct link to the resource, information, or website, you're mentioning, you make it easier for your readers to find the information and save them from having to search.

Posting Images

Images

 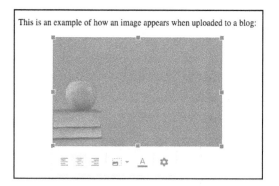

This is an example of how an image appears when uploaded to a blog:

Click on the Insert
Image button

To edit an image,
click on the image.

Image Posting

To post a photo on your blog, use the Insert Image icon in the WYSIWYG editor. When clicked, the icon will display the Add images dialog box with Upload selected. Click Choose File, then select the image to place on your blog post. Next, click on the Add Selected button.

Because of HTML limits, your placement is somewhat limited to what's possible using the WYSIWYG editor, so your options for positioning are left, center, or right of the text.

Image Editing in Blogger

Click on the image button to select it and bring up the image edit menu. Use the menu options to edit your image's appearance and other features using the menu options listed.

These options are:

- Resize the image
- Position the image to be left, center, or right of the text
- Add a caption
- Properties that can add and edit a hypertext link and add "alt" text.
- Remove deletes the image from your post.

Alt-text is important for two reasons. First, the alt text is used for assistive technology, or for situations when the image cannot appear on a user's web browser. Second, search engines use the alt text to identify the image content and log it for their index.

Video Posting

Video

Click on the Insert Video button

Upload a video from your computer or select one from YouTube

To post or embed a video, you usually need to host your video on another website like YouTube. Still, since Google owns both Blogger and YouTube, Google will let you upload videos directly to Blogger.

To insert a video, click on the Video button in the WYSIWYG editor, then upload it from your computer or click on the YouTube button, which opens the Add a Video screen where you can search for your videos or others on YouTube.

For most other blogging tools, you'll need to host your video on another video content site. Video files are huge, which makes it expensive for most blogging sites to host video directly. YouTube is the most often used service for hosting video since it's free. The Insert Video dialog on Blogger is similar to the Image dialog window and shows the options for selecting your video source.

In this example, I've chosen to embed a YouTube video. Searching for a video on YouTube, I found the one I wanted to use in the blog post, then copied the URL of the YouTube page and pasted it into the search box.

After clicking on the video to select it, the video appears on the blog post with the play arrow. A viewer can play the video from the blog.

While it's possible to search YouTube from within the insert video button, I found it easier to look for the video I want to post on YouTube, then copy and paste the link in the search box as shown below the video.

The term "embedded" is used to describe how video appears when a visitor to a web page clicks on the video's play icon (usually an arrow) to play it. With an embedded video, the video plays when a user clicks on the play button, without opening a new window or web page.

Video Appearance in a Post

Blogger Administration

Each blog is managed from your Blogger dashboard. There are many settings and options in the left column navigation, but you only need to setup a few of them, then you can concentrate on adding posts to your blog.

Blogger Administration

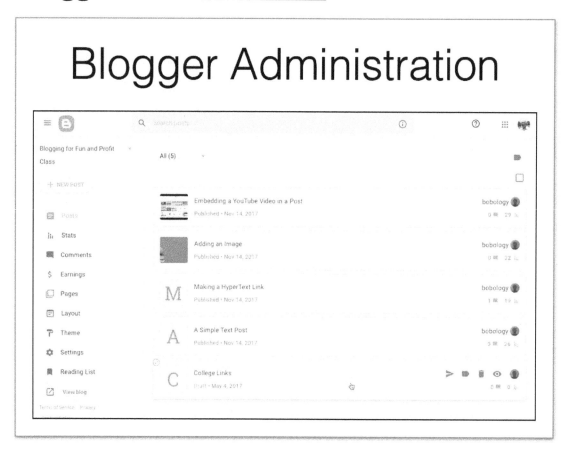

Whenever returning to Blogger, you'll see the most recent blog selected and the administrative options for that blog. Each blog you create on blogger is a separate website, but you manage them using one login. Since all the administrative options are the same for every blog, once you're familiar with them, you'll be able to use them on any blog you create and use on blogger.

Since all the administrative options are the same for every blog, once you're familiar with them you'll be able to use them on any blog you create and use on Blogger. Let's go over the administrative option menu on the left and then we'll look at some of the settings you may want to change.

Let's go over the administrative option menu on the left, and then we'll look at some of the settings you may want to change.

- Posts - Shows a view of all of your posts organized by All, Draft, and Published. Includes a search box for searching for any word in a post.

- Stats - shows basic statistics such as page views by date, time, posts, sources, and country. Includes statistics for pageviews by the type of browser and operating system.

- Comments - shows published, spam, and comments awaiting moderation.

- Earnings - sign up for displaying Google ads on your site to earn money.

- Campaigns - purchase ads from Google to promote your blog.

- Pages - create individual pages for your site. A page is different from a post and does not create an RSS broadcast but can display the same information. Pages are useful for a contact us form, shopping cart, directions, and hours, and each page has its own URL. Use Pages for content that's not likely to change often, such as a privacy policy, contact form, or shopping cart.

- Layout - add, edit, remove and reposition gadgets.

- Theme - change background, fonts, colors, layout, and more customization options.

- Settings - manage options for how your blog functions, including domain name, privacy, how posts are displayed, language, formatting, and more for advanced options.

- Reading List - view Blogger blogs you have added to your reading list. Usually includes news from Blogger, but you can subscribe to any Blogger site.

Help

The Help icon with the question mark gives you access to a rich library of information on how to use Blogger.

Advanced Analytics

Since Google owns Blogger, it comes with a subset of Google Analytics, one of the most widely used analysis tools for web traffic. Statistics will help you determine what content attracts the largest audience and what they like to come to your blog to see. You can read the article on Google Analytics on my website at this link: https://www.bobology.com/public/What-is-Google-Analytics.cfm.

Blogger Administration - Basic Settings

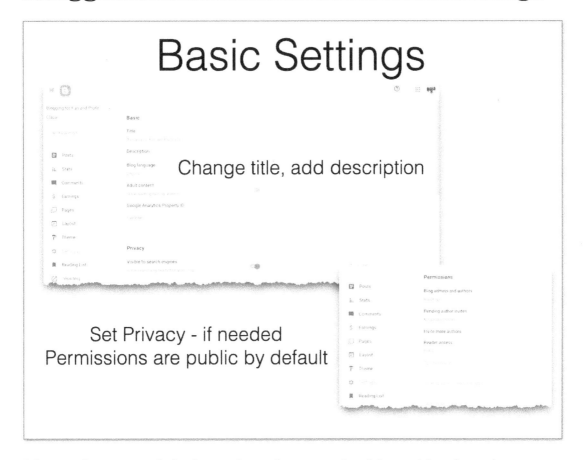

Blogger has some default settings that you should consider changing immediately for privacy and control over your blog content.

You can open the Settings page by clicking the "Settings" link in the left column. Hover over a setting to click on it, or move the selector button if the setting has an on or off option. Always check for a Save option for any setting you want to change.

For professional or business blogs, I recommend that you start with settings that won't list your blog or let search engines find it until you're ready to make your site public using the same setting changes for creating the Test blog we did earlier.

Until you start posting content, you don't have anything for visitors to read or view, so even if you draw them in with a great title, and you won't keep them interested. After you have content posted on your blog, and you're more familiar with Blogger, then change these settings back to their defaults. I recommend about 10-15 posts before promoting your blog.

Changing Your Blogger Domain Name

In Basic Settings, Publishing is used to change the blogspot.com subdomain URL or assign your own domain name to your blog. When creating the first blog earlier in this book, we used a domain name that included blogspot.com when we first set up a blog. Blogger allows you to change the subdomain name, which is the name used in front of ".blogspot.com."

You can point your existing domain name registered with another service to your Blogger blog, and it will override the .blogspot subdomain you used. Whenever people go to your domain name URL address, they will be directed to your blog on Blogger, but never see the name Blogspot anywhere. Domains can be registered with many services, and you can host your website anywhere. Just point your domain to your hosting location.

If you want to assign an existing domain, you can click the "Setup a 3rd party URL for your blog" link. You'll need to change some settings called "DNS" with your domain registrar following the instructions provided when you click "View Settings Instructions" then "Connect to your non-Google domain from Blogger." Your domain registrar help desk can help you make these changes and will walk you through the steps. I recommend printing out the instructions from Blogger to have them ready.

The alternative to pointing a 3rd party domain to your blog is to purchase a domain from Google. Google will automatically change the .blogspot subdomain to your new domain name. Domain registration isn't necessary but helps create a brand name that you can promote to people. If you plan on promoting yourself or a brand, you'll want to start with a domain name sooner since it will be the URL you use for marketing. You can move your website to another service, and Google will allow you to point your domain name to any location you choose for hosting.

Reader Access

The standard setting is Public, so your blog is on the web as soon as you create it. Changing permissions is important if you want to manage your blog's privacy. It's where you control adding additional authors to your blog and, more importantly, where you control who can read and see your blog. To allow anybody to read your blog means everyone on the World Wide Web, or in other words, anyone with access to the internet can find and read your blog.

You can limit your blog readers to people you choose using the Custom Readers option, which requires that you invite them by email. Selecting this option brings up a window to enter the email addresses of people you want to invite. Once entered, Blogger will send out an email invitation, which asks them to sign in with their Google ID or create one if they don't have one. Only the people you invited will be allowed to view your blog, and they will be asked to log in whenever they go to your Blogger URL.

Private to Authors allows you to invite people to write their own posts on your blog through a process like the one above. Note that any reader who can view your blog will be able to comment on your posts, so this option is best for only very small or family blogs.

Blogger Administration - Managing Comments

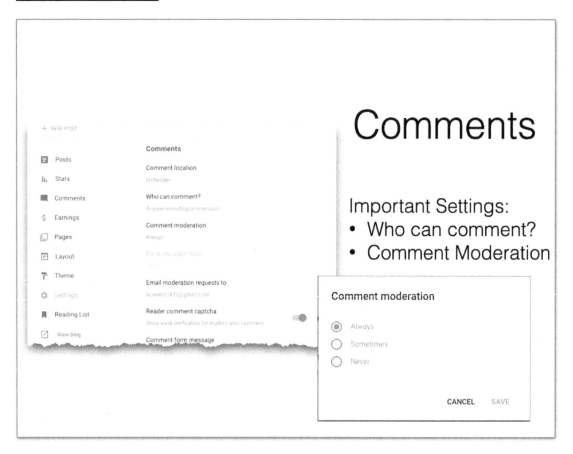

All blogs allow you to manage comments, the feedback that readers can attach to your posts. The most important settings for comments are Comment Location, Who Can Comment, and Comment Moderation.

Using "Comment Location," you can choose to show or hide comments for your entire blog, and if you choose to display comments, how the comments appear on your blog layout.

"Who Can Comment" determines what readers are allowed to comment and how they are required to identify themselves when they comment.

- Anyone – Meaning anyone visiting your blog can comment, and they don't have to identify themselves.

- Users with Google Accounts - This only lets someone comment after logging in with their Google account. I recommend either this option or the "Registered Users" setting since Google has Acceptable Use policies that a user would not want to break in making an inappropriate comment on a Blogger blog.

- Only Members of this Blog - This allows only people you have invited to be members of the blog to comment.

- You also have the option to turn comments off for a particular post in the WYSIWYG editor. Using this option, you can be selective in choosing which posts you want to allow comments on..

Moderating Comments

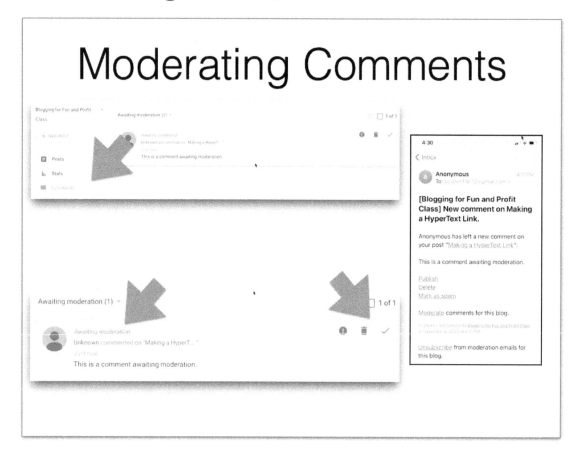

Comment moderation in a blog is different from allowing comments. Moderating comments is the way you can review and select those comments you approve to be displayed. Any comments by any authorized commenter will be immediately displayed without moderation turned on.

I always recommend using moderation set to "Always." Moderation means that the reader can comment, but the comment is held for your review before it appears on your blog.

To set Comment Moderation, click on Comment Moderation, then select the Always radio button. Now every comment will require approval before it is displayed on your blog. Selecting Sometimes sets up comment moderation for posts based on their age, as blog spammers tend to place comments on older posts because they know those posts aren't monitored as closely for new comments.

Entering an email address to receive a notification message is something I recommend as practical and useful. With email notification, whenever a comment is made, you'll automatically get an email from your blog letting you know when you have a comment. Then you know you'll need to review and approve a comment as quickly as possible. If you do receive a comment, be sure to approve it as soon as possible, generally within 24 hours or sooner. If you like the comment and have something to add, you can also reply to the comment.

Other Types of Blogging

Some forms of blogging use video and audio content. Let's take a look at some options.

<u>Video Blogging</u>

YouTube is the best-known video blogging site and has made it easy for people to publish videos. Video blogging is made easy with tools for uploading and converting video from almost any source, including cell phones. You can start a YouTube channel for free, but they control the advertising on the site.

Twitter, Instagram, and Facebook, and other social networks support video posting. Another popular video hosting site is Vimeo.

YouTube users can post episodes like a television show or mini-series, and create a channel, much like a television channel, that users can subscribe to and receive notifications when new episodes are posted.

YouTube and video have become powerful ways to communicate content. If you aren't comfortable making your video, you can hire a professional to make your video.

Video production may seem intimidating at first, but you can create quality videos with a little effort. For many people, recording themselves on video, doing interviews, or providing how-to instruction on a topic is a more comfortable way of communicating than writing.

The secret to a good video is quality sound and a script. While many videos on YouTube appear casual, almost every video is shot with a script and is rehearsed. Smartphone cameras are perfect for recording the video image, but you'll want an accessory microphone to obtain higher quality sound.

A good resource for product recommendations I use is wirecutter.com. Just search for microphones.

YouTube offers a chance for popular channels to make money by letting YouTube run ads, but you need 1,000 subscribers and a minimum number of hours of video views to qualify.

Vimeo is a popular video hosting service for people who want to create a paid channel or restrict access to members or subscribers.

You can read more about video content in my book "Introduction to Internet Marketing Methods."

Audio and Podcasts

iTunes is the home of podcasting, where you can find and publish audio and video content on just about any topic. Most blogging software makes podcasting easy to do, allowing you to embed an audio file in your blog. However, Blogger doesn't have any built-in podcasting features, but you can embed a podcast on a post much like you embed a video.

Podcasting Services

TypePad is one of the easiest blogs for podcasts and includes an audio file upload link in their WYSIWYG editor. Other blogs can support audio files using a plugin or HTML option from an audio hosting service. Two popular ones are Libsyn and Blubrry.

These services start at about $5 a month, store all of your podcast episodes, and have extensive help.

- lybsyn.com
- blubrry.com

Spotify has a new free podcasting service called anchor.fm which has tools for creating a podcast using only a smartphone.

What you can do with podcasting.

Podcasting is a way of making an audio broadcast available for download, either as a single broadcast or a series where people can subscribe to periodic episodes.

A subscription to a podcast channel allows the listener to get automatic downloads from iTunes when a new episode is available. The episode is downloaded to their smartphone and available for them to listen to at their convenience. Radio stations such as National Public Radio, commentators, and others use iTunes podcasting, bloggers, and businesses that use podcasting for promotional purposes.

To do podcasting, you need an audio recording, which you then post to your blog. Once you have your audio post, register your blog with iTunes, and the updated podcasts are made available as you post them on your blog. Apple reviews every podcast before placing it on iTunes. All podcasts on iTunes are free and include a wide range of topics, including news, current events, and brand name podcasts for product or brand marketing. Podcasts are a very effective and inexpensive way to build your audience.

You can create an audio file from many sources. You can make recordings with your computer or a digital recorder and then edit or mix them before posting them. Editing audio is important to select the portion of the recording you want to use, remove silence, add sound effects—Mac's come standard with GarageBand, which has a built-in podcasting option.

PC users can download the free Audacity software at www.audacity.com, allowing you to create audio files suitable for iTunes.

Microphones

I recommend using an external microphone and not the internal microphone on your computer. Internal microphones are usually not very high quality, and audio quality is important. A USB microphone or lavalier microphone will make a great improvement in your recording quality. As I mentioned earlier, wirecutter.com is a resource I use for recommendations, but I personally use a Yeti Blue microphone for my recording.

An excellent resource for learning more about podcasting is listening to podcasts about podcasting on iTunes.

You Are a Publisher

By placing content on the Internet, you are now publishing content. With any publication, you have legal rights and legal issues you need to be aware of as a publisher and author.

We have a free press in the United States, but it has limits and responsibilities. If you slander or defame someone's character, you run the risk of a civil lawsuit, so be careful what you say. Think of anything that would damage someone's personal or business reputation, but don't be afraid, to be honest about facts and events that occur or that you want to communicate. Be careful when expressing your opinions and being critical in a malicious manner.

Copyright law protects the use of any copyrighted content by the author or publisher, and you should post a copyright notice on your blog to protect yourself. Using anyone else's content, be it text, graphic, or video, can be a violation of copyright. Media companies have resources that monitor the use of their copyrighted and trademarked property.

There is a way you can use excerpts of copyrighted material, but be cautious. It's the "fair use" policy.

Copyright and Fair Use

Copyright – Fair Use

- Fair use is a "doctrine" not a law:

- "Section 107 contains a list of the various purposes for which the reproduction of a particular work may be considered "fair," such as criticism, comment, news reporting, teaching, scholarship, and research."

http://www.copyright.gov/fls/fl102.html

Fair use is not a law but a set of case law that has resulted from court cases involving copyrighted material for critical use or review. For example, a movie critic can't very well review a movie unless he can use the title, and if it's a broadcast, the critic may want to use a scene from the movie to make a point in his or her review. I'm not a lawyer, and this isn't a legal opinion. If you are in doubt, consult an attorney.

In general, you can use excerpts from a copyrighted work, but it depends on your user's purpose. For example, using screenshots from some of the websites I used in this book and for my class is considered fair use for teaching. To teach the topic, I use screenshots of certain web pages as illustrations to make a point. Fair use allows using a certain amount of copyright material, usually for education, commentary, criticism, or review of the material. It would be best if you strived to use the minimum amount of material necessary to make your point. If necessary, you can link to the original content on the web, which is perfectly acceptable since you are only referencing the content and not publishing it on your website.

Fair use is a "doctrine," not a law:

> ***"Section 107 contains a list of the various purposes for which the reproduction of a particular work may be considered "fair," such as criticism, comment, news reporting, teaching, scholarship, and research."***

The U.S. Copyright Office has a link to fair use at http://www.copyright.gov/fls/fl102.html, but when in doubt about using material from another website or publication, consult an attorney. Specific situations vary, and you should read any copyright or usage information on any material before using it in your blog. Here is the link to the U.S. Copyright Office and Fair Use reference:

Under no circumstances should you ever make someone else's copyrighted material available to copy or reproduce unless it's your own material. If in doubt, be sure to consult an attorney.

Creating Content

Creating content

- How long should a post be?

- How often should I post?

- What do I post about?

- Link to other web sites and blogs

- Put images and photos on your posts

Creating content for your blog should focus most of your time and attention since the content will be what readers find most valuable. Understanding your readers and audience and what value you bring to them with your content is important if you are interested in increasing your blog readership. Increasing the traffic to your blog or any website is the focus of Internet marketing and outside this book's scope. If you're interested in learning more, I cover internet marketing in my book on "Introduction to Internet Marketing Methods," available on my website.

Content Style, Length, and Frequency

Think about your post's length and what readers of your blog site will see when they view your Home page. Showing the entire text of a post on your blog may result in only one article and it's headline appearing for a reader. The reader may conclude that you only have one article on your blog, as most computer users don't scroll down when viewing web pages. Keep this in mind when writing posts.

One solution is to write short blog articles to see several headlines and articles on a page. But a better solution is to use the Page Break feature in the WYSIWYG editor of most blogs (including Blogger) to break up a post. Position your cursor in the second or third line of text or after an image, then click on the Page Break symbol. A break is inserted in your blog post, and your Home page will show the headline and the content before your break. A link is automatically inserted so a reader can click and view a webpage with the entire post.

In general, a 500-word blog post is a good guideline for the length of a text article. If interested, people will take the time to read a 500-word article. Inserting an image or photo adds visual interest, and almost every professional blog uses an image or photo in each post.

If you don't know where to find photos, use some of the stock photo and image websites where you can legally obtain the use of images.

Here's a link to my blog post on finding stock photos:

https://www.bobology.com/public/What-are-Stock-Photos.cfm

People don't need to see new content every minute of the day for frequency, but going a month without a post is a long time for a blog. Twice a week is a good schedule to plan for your blog, but if you're able to add content more frequently, that's better. Establishing a regular schedule for posting is important, and your readers will come to expect your posts and look forward to them once you establish a schedule.

Content isn't just limited to text and words. As a blogger, think about your reader and what they could use. Hypertext links, images, maps, photos, and video are all usable content for your blog and maybe easier for you to create depending on your style and your blog's focus..

Quality Posting

Quality Posting

- Vocabulary - use what's natural

- Style - Strunk & White

- Grammar: www.grammarly.com

- Check facts before you post

- Outsource:

    - textbroker.com

    - zerys.com

    - iwriter.com

A well-written copy is read more often and more easily than a poorly written copy. You may already be an accomplished writer, or you may be starting and need to acquire some basic skills. Professional writing skills aren't required, but some basics can improve the quality of your content.

Improving Your Writing

Use your own vocabulary and be as natural as possible. Proofread everything at least once, preferably twice, before you decide to post it to your blog. Misspelled words and poor grammar will negatively affect people's impression of your content and distract from the message.

Style guides like Strunk & White's "The Elements of Style" are good tools for any writer. A style guide helps you be consistent in your writing and use names, terms, abbreviations, punctuation, and follow grammar usage rules.

An excellent online grammar tool is Grammarly, which I use for my writing. It checks grammar, spelling, and usage and can improve your writing skills rapidly. You can find it at www.grammarly.com.

All blogging software allows you to cut and paste copy from another application into your editor, and writing in another application may be more comfortable for you. If you use any facts or data, quotes, or other specific information, double-check them before making your post. Fact-checking is an important part of writing, and blog reputations can be built on good, accurate information.

And if you need help with content, you can purchase articles from sites like Textbroker (www.textbroker.com), Zerys (www.zerys.com), and iWriter (www.iwriter.com).

Photo and Graphic Editors

Photo and Graphic Editing Tools

Three most common needs for bloggers:
- Resize
- Crop
- Annotate with text and icons

Note: Included with TypePad

Photos and graphics can be uploaded from files on your computer in all blogging software. Look for a photo icon on your WYSIWYG editor. There are many different types of graphics files, though, and the most commonly used ones for the web are png, jpeg, and gif.

TypePad includes the Aviary photo editor as standard with the TypePad WYSIWYG editor, which offers powerful photo editing options.

Most of the time, you'll want to do a few basic tasks which will cover almost all of your photo and image editing requirements. These are:

- resize your photo to the exact dimensions for your blog post

- crop or trim unwanted portions of your photo or image

- add annotations such as text or arrows to highlight or explain items in your image

Adobe's Photoshop application is the #1 commercial software used for photo and graphics editing. It's extremely functional, but it can take a while to learn.

An alternative to Photoshop is GIMP, which is a Photoshop-like free, open-source software with almost as much functionality as Photoshop.

The latest version of Office with PowerPoint comes with a built-in graphics and photo editor and may give you enough options for your needs. Mac users have access to photo and graphic editing tools using the built-in Preview application.

You can download photo and graphics editors at the following websites:

- GIMP - www.gimp.org
- Canva - www.canva.com

More Ideas for Posts

Getting ideas for posts

- News articles

- Conversations with people

- Anything you read

- Places you go

- Things you do

- Make notes and keep ideas handy

Tell a story where readers have to come back to get the next part. Cliffhangers on television shows work for a reason. Don't be afraid to use this technique yourself. Invite comments to your blog and respond quickly if necessary, so people will know you're active.

Keep a notebook and jot down ideas as you think of them. Before long, you'll have a list of topics for blog articles. Think about what interests you daily. Trying to create a blog about something you don't care much about is a sure way to lose interest (as well as not have any fun!).

Use these ideas for creating variety in your content:

- Posts with links to other websites, articles, blogs:

- Use screen captures when referencing other websites.

- Consider reader surveys and publish the feedback.

- Invite comments by asking for them in a specific post.

- Use maps, images, graphics, video, audio to add visual interest to your blog.

- Tell a story with a multi-part post, just like a mini-series would do with multiple episodes.

Scheduled Posting

All blogs allow you to schedule posts. If you are away for a week and want to post daily, you can create each day's post and schedule them for posting. It's a good idea to have a calendar schedule to make sure you post regularly. Writing and creating several posts at once is a good way to make sure you're regularly posting.

Email posting

Almost any blog allows you to send an email to your blog and have it automatically post. If you have access to email, you can post whenever you can send one, even from your cell phone. Every cell phone account has an email address for sending emails (different from text messaging), and you can attach photos in the email for posting with the text copy.

Mobile Posting

Mobile apps are available for most blogging tools like Blogger, WordPress and others for smartphones and tablets.

Multiple Authors

If you have someone who shares your interest in the blog, consider allowing multiple authors. You can each create content, like a newspaper with multiple columnists.

Using all of these ideas for posts will make it easier to add content to your blog and make it more interesting for your readers.

Making Money With Your Blog

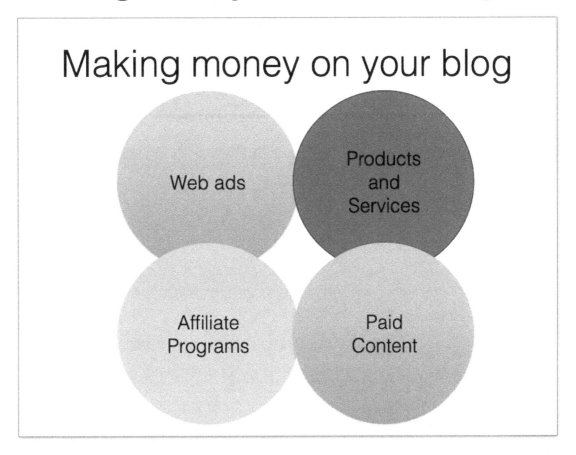

There are four main ways to make money from blogging; web ads, affiliate programs, paid content and selling products or services with e-commerce. With millions of bloggers on the Internet, you can access a wide range of resources and tools for generating income from your blog.

If your primary goal is to make money with blogging, think about which of these approaches you might want to pursue, either alone or as a combination. Let's review each of these and see how they work and what you need to use them.

Advertising Income

Advertising

Google AdSense

blogger gadget

http://www.google.com/adsense/

Google AdSense

Blogger makes it easy to make money with the world's largest web advertising company, Google. With just a few clicks, you can add Google ads to your blog using the Google AdSense program. One reason why Google encourages blogging with a free Blogger account is to make more money from advertising. With more places to place ads (like blogs), Google makes more money from the advertisers, who use Ads to purchase pay-per-click advertising.

When a person uses Google to search for something on the web, they type in a word or phrase. The word or phrase is called a keyword. Google keeps an index of the internet and the content on each site. After the keyword is entered and the user clicks on "search," Google produces a search result page. This page includes some sites that Google decides are relevant to the user's search and advertisements, usually small text ads at the top or on the side of the page. These ads are paid for by advertisers who want their ads to appear when someone types in a specific keyword search term.

When someone clicks on one of these ads, Google makes money. Google's AdSense program is how you can display ads from Google on your blog. You get paid when someone clicks on an ad that's displayed by Google on your blog. The click fee is deposited in your account and paid when you reach a minimum amount of revenue, usually $100.00.

If you do the math, to make $1,000 a month on your blog from web ads would require having 20,000 clicks at 5 cents a click. Don't be discouraged, though, as there are thousands of sites making money. Google is a multi-billion dollar company because people click on the ads that advertisers buy. Google AdSense is free to anyone with a website, regardless of the traffic and volume. There is no minimum amount of traffic you need to have for your blog, and the AdSense program is free to join.

Self-hosted Ads

Some Bloggers sell their own advertising space directly to advertisers. I've seen PTA groups use this approach to place a sponsor ad for a month or a year in a gadget or banner and cover the hosting cost. It's your publication. If you have a specific niche market appeal to an audience, this approach can effectively make money, particularly with local and small businesses trying to reach a targeted audience. Be sure to draw up an advertising contract, and I recommend collecting payment in advance.

Setting Up Google AdSense

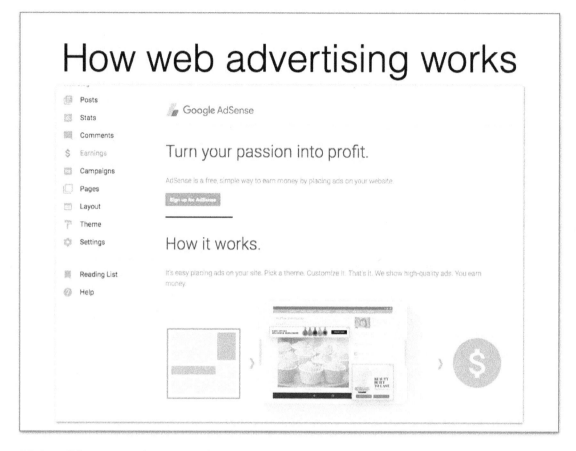

Using Blogger, where you have your first blog site, is the easiest way to start selling ads. Google has an "Earnings" link in the Administration column.

You'll need a U.S. tax identification (social security or EIN), a checking account, and the bank routing number.

Google will walk you step by step in setting up your AdSense account almost as easy as setting up your blog. Remember, you make money when Google makes money, so you're partners with them with AdSense.

Google searches your web site (remember to make it public and searchable) and uses keywords to decide what ads to display. If you have content on cars, you'll get car-related ads, content on finance, finance-related ads, etc.

You can use your AdSense account on any website or blog you create. There is no need to create a separate account, but you need to register any additional websites for Google to index and track the ads.

Affiliate Programs

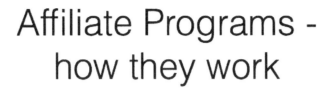

 www.affiliate-program.amazon.com/

 www.marketing.rakuten.com/affiliate-marketing

www.linkconnector.com/

 www.clickbank.com/

 www.cj.com/

Affiliate programs allow you to refer people to a product, service, or other item and get paid when someone buys that item or service. They range from software to books to home loans and have payout fees based on a referral from your web site. When you join an affiliate program, you get an account that creates a cookie, then copy and paste your affiliate link HTML code on your blog (instead of a standard hypertext link) to take a reader to a page with a product or service.

You are a "referring" website, and the affiliate company knows the referral came from you because of the cookie. I recommend starting with Amazon's affiliate program since it's easy, and more than likely, if you've ever bought anything on the web, you've probably bought something from Amazon.

Some companies have their own affiliate program, but many businesses use affiliate networks. You enroll in the network and then apply to be an affiliate in each sponsored program. Some advertiser programs automatically accept your application. Others require approval and review your website or blog to see if they want to include you in their network. Usually, the review is for appropriate content and audience.

Some of the most popular affiliate programs are:

- Amazon affiliates: https://affiliate-program.amazon.com
- Commission Junction: www.cj.com
- LinkShare: www.linkshare.com
- ClickBank: www.clickbank.com
- Linkconnector www.linkconnector.com

Except for Amazon, where all affiliate links are to Amazon products, the ones listed here are organizations that provide affiliate services and bring advertisers and publishers together.

If you're a "go-to" person for information or assistance on any topic, using affiliate programs can help generate income: the greater your site's traffic, the greater your affiliate program referrals. However, be careful not to oversell because your priority should be to provide quality content for your audience.

Using Affiliate Links

The affiliate advertiser provides a small piece of HTML code for your website or blog for you to use. This code includes your affiliate tracking cookie, which the advertiser and affiliate program uses to track the source of a referral.

The HTML code comes in a variety of formats. Some are text-only and display the product or service name in text. Some include an image or picture, and some are different sizes and shapes.

To use the HTML links, you copy the link and paste it into your blog editor using the HTML view, NOT the WYSIWYG view. Use your "test" blog and try out different HTML code from advertisers and paste it into your practice blog to see how it appears in a preview.

The next time you write a blog or post a photo of a product, remember to use an affiliate link to generate income from your advice and recommendations.

Your affiliate program will track your statistics, which are usually visible on a reporting screen you can view in your affiliate account. Advertisers and programs vary when they send money. Still, there is usually a minimum amount of affiliate income that has to be generated, from $25 to $100, before a check or deposit is made into your account.

Affiliate programs give you more precise control over the specific brands and products you show ads for on your site, and over 18,000 companies pay commissions.

Finding Affiliate Programs to Join

To find affiliate programs look in the fine print at the bottom of a website, search for an affiliate program for the brand you want to use, or search the affiliate management sites for advertisers by name or product type.

Paid Content

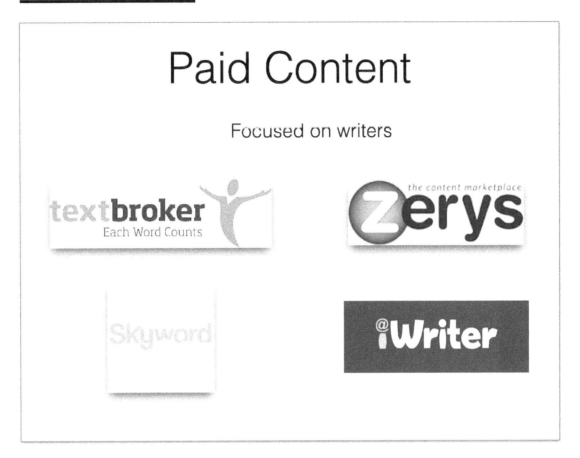

Blog Content Creation

Successful approaches to getting paid for your content all involve establishing yourself as an active Blogger. Creating and posting high quality, well-written articles, and content generate traffic and an audience. As your content grows, your audience will start to include people interested in the topics you write about. They will start recommending your blog to others, which will increase your audience.

At some point, as you become established as an expert or authority about your topics, your audience will include other Bloggers, journalists, media industry staff, and industry experts. There is a constant demand for new, well-written content on the web, and people need fresh content.

Search engine optimization service providers, businesses, and other organizations know that they need to update websites continuously. The larger the company, the more important it is to have frequently updated content. Businesses of all sizes are becoming more aware of the need to update content to communicate. By letting people know you're a blogger and content creator, you will find businesses contacting you to discuss creating a blog and social media content..

Writing Assignments

SEO companies, advertising agencies, and businesses use both full-time staff and freelancers for blogging and social media posting. They often use online writer's markets to source writers for their projects.

With the need to create content for social media, video, and websites, content creators with skill and expertise in any subject are in demand. There are two marketplaces for writers, U.S. based organizations that are looking for native English speaking writers with an understanding of context and general-purpose freelance sites that have a broad international writer community.

I recommend you focus on the U.S. based markets as they pay more. These marketplaces give writers a free account and usually ask for a sample of their writing. Your writing is graded, which determines the rate per-word you are paid for any assignment. You create a profile, similar to a social media profile, describing yourself and your subject area skills.

Once your profile is reviewed and posted, you can search for writing assignments to accept, and publishers can contact you through the marketplace to request a quote or assignment.

In most cases, your assignment is a short blog post on a specific topic, and the publisher will post guidelines for the article. You accept the assignment, then submit your work on the marketplace site for the publisher to review. Writers are required to make at least one set of editing requests, but the publisher does have the ability to react to your work if they don't find it acceptable. The marketplace has resolution policies and monitors publishers who make too many rejections to remove them from the service.

Once your article is accepted, you're paid. Publishers are required to deposit funds in advance of any work requests, and your payment is made through the site, so there's less risk of not being paid.

Writer's Marketplaces

You can register at these links:

- www.zerys.com
- www.textbroker.com
- www.skyword.com
- www.iwriter.com

You can post a profile and solicit and look for freelance work on sites such as www.upwork.com and www.freelancer. com, but these are more international in focus with more competition.

LinkedIn

Don't forget to update and complete your LinkedIn profile since many freelancers obtain work through it.

E-Commerce on Your Blog

Since a blog is a website, it's possible to sell your products and services on your blog. Blogger doesn't include a shopping cart or e-commerce function, but it's possible to include these functions within a blog without the need for a separate website or shopping cart site. Other services offer a way to add e-commerce capability to any blog or website, and some services include e-commerce functions as standard.

If you know from the start you're going to be selling products, look at Squarespace, Shopify, Wix, or Weebly, as they all have integrated shopping cart features. PayPal and SquareUp are excellent if you only have a few products or services.

PayPal www.paypal.com

PayPal has an easy way to create a seller account for free, charging only when a sale is made. You can create a new PayPal account or use your existing one, then register as a seller. PayPal gives you tools to create a product listing, prices, add shipping information, and process the payment. You get HTML code, so viewers see a "Buy Now" or 'Donate Now" button that takes them through the checkout process.

SquareUp www.squareup.com

SquareUp is a company that makes widely-used credit card readers. And they do a lot more. You can use your Square account to create a free online store and add products for sale on any website, similar to PayPal, and Square has a feature for appointment bookings. Square also owns Weebly.

SquareSpace www.squarespace.com

Squarespace includes a shopping cart and merchant processing with all plans, so you're ready to go with a shopping cart anytime. All business plans support digital downloads.

Shopify www.shopify.com

Squarespace includes a shopping cart and merchant processing with all plans, so you're ready to go with a shopping cart anytime. All business plans support digital downloads.

Wix and Weebly www.wix.com www.weebly.com

Squarespace includes a shopping cart and merchant processing with all plans, so you're ready to go with a shopping cart anytime. All business plans support digital downloads.

Woocommerce www.woocommerce.com

Probably the most popular shopping cart and e-commerce add-on for WordPress websites.

eBay

Has seller options based on volume and a feature for an eBay store. Handles the transaction and payment processing and takes a percentage for selling. You can link to your eBay products and store them from your blog using a hypertext link.

Amazon

Allows sales of individual products and a store option. Like eBay, you can link to your items from your blog. Amazon processes payments and takes a percentage for the listing.

For the most part, all commerce solutions are designed to handle physical products, digital products (for download), and services. Here are a few of the more common and simpler approaches available to a Blogger who wants to sell products and services from their blog.

Etsy

Etsy is a popular marketplace and it's possible to sell custom writing, design, and digital downloads.

Digital Products

Digital Goods, also referred to as virtual products, are available as files for download. eBooks, software, photos, artwork, video, music, and subscriptions are possible ideas for digital goods, all of which you can sell on your blog.

If virtual products are part of your e-commerce plan, you'll need to pay for a service that supports this. Squarespace, Wix, Weebly, and Shopify offer digital download e-commerce functionality. You can use a separate service that's integrated with PayPal for digital downloads.

Two popular services that offer economical digital download capacities that you can use on any website are PayLoadz www.payloadz.com and E-Junkie www.e-junkie.com.

Forms and Bookings

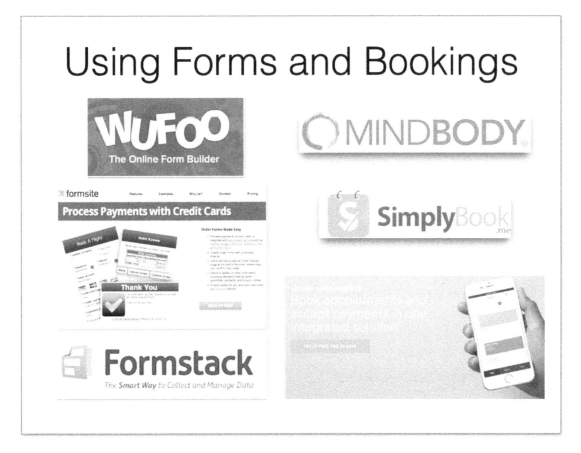

Many types of products and services are best sold on a blog by using a form. By using a form, a customer enters information in fields you create when you build the form. Within the form, you can include options that the customer selects for their purchase. Common options include a radio selection, a check box, or a drop-down list of items. These features offer more flexibility and choice for your products or services but don't make it too difficult for someone to complete the form.

Forms

Many form websites include an e-commerce function, host the form, and provide the blogger with cut and paste HTML code for embedding the form in their blog or website. Forms can be used to sell tickets, take orders, arrange for services, and link to virtual goods, in addition to purchasing physical products. Forms provide the ability to collect more data and offer more choices if necessary for your e-commerce goals.

Forms with e-commerce capabilities are a hosted service and generally require a small monthly or annual fee. Some popular form sites with e-commerce capability are:

- Formstack   www.formstack.com
- Wufoo   www.wufoo.com
- Formsite   www.formsite.com

Booking and Appointment Setting

Businesses and people in personal services like hairstylists, personal trainers, tutors, repair, etc.. rely on appointments and their time for making money. Booking and appointment setting tools provide the convenience of online booking through the web or a mobile app along with the ability to accept payment in advance.

All of these tools can be integrated into a blog with cut and paste HTML code. Some popular booking and appointment sites are:

- Mindbody - www.software.mindbodtonline.com
- SimplyBook www.simplybook.me
- Square Appointments www.squareup.com/appointments

Business Blogging

If you're creating a blog for a business, it's important to have an objective and goal for your blog. You're making an impression, and as the adage goes, first impressions count. You may never get a second chance, considering how quickly a mouse click takes! Planning is more important since you have a reputation to maintain, and your content has to reflect and add value to your business. It helps to have clear goals and objectives for a business blog. Here are some ideas for focus:

- Lead generation
- New products
- Showcase expertise
- Employee communication
- Customer support

Your blog should have a specific business goal. Don't be afraid of specializing it too much and create multiple blogs if it makes sense. Blogs are inexpensive compared to websites. Remember, if the content isn't worthwhile, it doesn't matter who it's targeted for. People will stop reading it.

Here are eight steps for effective business blogging you can follow:

1. Set a goal for your blog.
2. Commit to maintaining it.
3. Focus on the content.
4. Target your audience and find out what people want.
5. Ask others for ideas and help.
6. Plan out a month's worth of posts in advance.
7. Edit and proofread everything at least 2x.
8. Use keywords in your blog posts.

Promoting Your Blog

When your blog is ready to promote, focus on a regular posting schedule, and add content. Your content is your most valuable resource and provides the highest value for your readers. When you're ready to start promoting your blog, these are some of the most common ways Bloggers promote their sites:

- Allow search engines to find it.
- Invite comments.
- Use social media sites to increase traffic.
- Post consistently.
- Add your blog URL to your email signature.
- Add your blog URL to any printed or collateral items you use for promotion.
- Buy PPC Ads.
- Offer an email list subscription.

Visit other blog sites related to yours, make a comment, and you're likely to get one or more of the authors of that blog visiting your site. If your blog is interesting and offers some benefit for their readers, they might link to one of your articles or reference your blog in a post. One sure thing, if you don't comment, they won't know you have a blog.

Leverage Social Media Contacts

If you have a network of friends on Facebook or another social media site, be sure to let them know about your blog. You can make posts on Facebook or Twitter and link back to your blog to attract readership. Refer to the RSS section for more information on how to do this and using tools like dlvr. It, Buffer and Hootsuite.

Using an audience, you may already have in place on a social site, you can bring them to your blog for additional content if they are interested in reading or learning more.

Email Signatures

Every email you send out is an opportunity to promote your blog. Gmail, Hotmail, Yahoo Mail, Outlook, and almost any other email program has an option for adding a signature to your email. A signature is a block of text or graphics that your email software automatically puts on every outgoing email.

Be sure to add a message like "read my blog" in addition to your blog URL, so people know what you want from them.

Post on a Schedule

Very few bloggers actually post regularly. A daily post is considered frequent, while every other week is considered a long gap. About two posts a week on your blog will be adequate, and if you get a chance, more often will increase readership. Invite comments to build community, post regularly, and focus on your content, and you'll be an accomplished blogger!

Additional Resources

As a purchaser of this book, you receive a free 365 day account with access to the bobology.com training website. Use this account for access to additional articles, videos, software, and training materials to stay up to date.

Here's what you'll receive with your 365 day free access:

Exclusive Access to Class Section - access to the class section of the website for updates to the workbook and additional information only available to members

Technology Explanations - using the same style and approach used in my classes, with clear, easy-to-understand information.

Discussion Forum Moderated by Bob Cohen - answers to *your* questions from Bob and his own advisors in this exclusive members-only forum.

Downloadable Copies of Class Slides

Access to Newsletter Archives

Member-Only Training Events

Document and Software Downloads

Here's how to setup your free account:

1. Go to www.bobology.com

2. Scroll down on your browser until you see the blue Promo Code box in the right column (at the bottom of the mobile app)

3. Enter the promo code **BLOG15**

4. Complete the registration form on the next web page

5. Confirm your membership email subscription

6. Log in to the Members only area with your member username and password

Add yourself to the newsletter for announcements, webinars, and more!